SCILL
BUILDING H

Peter Mad

ıgustus Smith, the son of a
ily. The self-styled 'Lord
as a benevolent dictator,
s over the years including
extensive rebuilding of
l as introducing universal
its to fishing, farming and
; were continued by his
), realising the advantages
duced the early flowers
stant city markets on the
/ then, in the last century,
ı a subsistence existence
ns.

erted to the Duchy of
Smith family still lease the
n active part in island life,
ince the 1830s.

islands have generally
naking an important
omy alongside the flower
dings are now recognised
and architectural interest
ases, buildings from all
e and conservation in the
res for development and
trictly controlled, and the
more than that of a large
helping to maintain the
s of Scilly.

MATERIALS AND WORKMANSHIP

Historically, local granite has been predominantly used for the construction of all types of buildings on Scilly, from burial chambers and cottages to farm-houses and public institutions. In most of England stone was normally reserved for important projects, particularly where other traditional materials such as bricks or timber were readily available. The majority of the domestic buildings on Scilly were built with the brown granite from which the islands were formed, as in the highland areas of Devon and Cornwall. At one time there was a plentiful supply of quarried rock or moorstone on the islands whereas other materials were scarce. Eventually, by 1883, when St Mary's new church, pier and large houses had been constructed, not half of the stone required was available on the islands and a substantial amount had to be imported from Cornwall. Even by 1852, when Bishop Rock lighthouse was re-built, granite had been imported from quarries at Carnsew, near Mabe in Cornwall. Granite is virtually indestructible and had been used some 2,500-4,000 years ago for building massive masonry tombs on the islands to house the dead. It was also used for stone hedges to provide protection from the strong gales. Apart from its reassuring strength and durability, it has an attractive appearance with subtle variations in texture and colour. Its disadvantages are that it is not easy to work and therefore cutting and

Moorstone granite, Bronze Age Dwellings, Nonour

Granite ashlar, Hugh Street, St Mary's

shaping are difficult and decoration is rare, and its porous nature leads to problems of dampness. Better property would be plastered internally while lime mortar and a coloured or natural lime wash externally could reduce the damp problem. Normally the rough faced granite would be laid in courses, or at least laid roughly in courses. In the case of more important buildings the granite was finely-cut and laid accurately in courses with close joints. This technique is known as ashlar.

Dry stone walling - that is, without mortar - would be used for unimportant outbuildings or stone hedges. At one time, stones were often bedded in natural red gritty clay or 'ram' and the and gaps between the boulders filled with small stones or rubble. Later, improved joints were formed using lime-sand mortar or cement-sand mortar. A very fine sand was obtained from Porthmellon Beach on St Mary's whilst lime and cement were imported. An unusual use of granite can be seen at the Post Office in Hugh Town on St Mary's and at the porches to the cottages at New Grimsby on Tresco, where massive chunks of stone were used creating strong patterns of light and shade across the face of the walls.Bricks were rare due to the high cost of importing them and usually reserved for chimney stacks. An exception, in about 1930, is the use of small grey concrete bricks for the houses at Porthcressa Terrace in Hugh Town, St Mary's

Roughly coursed stone walling to the old pier at St Mary's

Rough blocks of granite to cottage porch at New Grimsby, Tresco.

and a row of houses at Higher Town on St Martins.

Timber which had been washed ashore from wrecks was used for buildings when available, but most structural timber which was used for rafters, purlins, beams and joists came from the mainland. Sometimes, quantities of oak, mahogany and teak became available from wrecks.

The traditional roofing material was reeds which were used for thatch. In 1669, Count Lorenzo Magalotti, a visitor to the islands, reported that he found the houses low but in other respects resembling the buildings of England, being made of excellent material. A few were slate roofed at that time but the more common ones had 'a peculiar sort of covering by way of a roof having nothing but a simple mat spread over the rafters and drawn tight all round.' Subsequently this form of roof

Grey concrete bricks and small Delabole roof slates used at Porthcressa Terrace.

Natural slate roof at Bryher

Double Roman clay tiles used on roof of an outbuilding to a house on the Parade, St Mary's

covering was superseded by the use of thatch which was a distinct improvement. Until the last century buildings in exposed positions had their thatch secured by straw ropes which were used to protect against riffling in stormy weather. The ropes were crossed in a chequer- board pattern and either secured with stones to weight them down or fastened to iron or wooden pegs driven into chinks in the walls about 18 inches below eaves level. At one time, the plaiting of these straw ropes was an Old Town industry on St Mary's. These type of thatched roofs were also used in other exposed areas such as Ireland and Scotland. Thatched roofs have now all disappeared on Scilly, the last one, on a cottage at Tresco, having been re-roofed with slates in 1989-90. Slates, imported from the mainland, became more common for roofs in the 19th and 20th centuries. The Delabole smalls or peggies were frequently used on the islands; they are particularly attractive and appropriate for Scilly. A coat of cement slurry has sometimes been applied to slate roofs for additional protection against the elements although this mars their appearance. Bridgwater double Roman red clay pantiles were also imported from the mainland in the mid-19th century and used throughout the islands. Today there are a variety of modern roof coverings including cement slates, cedar shingles, corrugated asbestos, steel, plain and interlocking concrete tiles, asphalt and bituminous felt. Although many of these materials are economical, aesthetically they are most unsatisfactory since they lack the richness of colour, texture and weathering properties of natural materials. This is particularly important at Scilly where roofs are often viewed from higher ground and dominate the scene. This problem is further accentuated by the increased use of plastics for windows and rainwater

'Thatch' cottage at Tresco. Last building on Scilly to have retained its thatched roof, re-roofed with 20th century slates between 1989-90.

goods on buildings with simple forms, where attention to detail and reliance on the character of natural materials is of paramount importance.

Nowadays, architects are often concerned with the sustainability of the built environment. This may involve re-cycling materials or finding new uses for existing buildings. Scillonians have been re-claiming materials from exhausted buildings, shipwrecks and even ancient burial mounds for centuries; the re-use of stone is a common occurrence at Scilly. Numerous examples include Star Castle, some of the cottages at Old Town and Cromwell Castle, which used granite taken from the ruins of older castles at St Mary's and Tresco. Stones from the dismantled Windmill at Peninnis Head were believed to have been employed to repair Old Town Quay in the 19th century and the extension to the pier on St Mary's between 1820-90 is reputed to have been partly built using shaped stones from barrows.

Timber, re-claimed from older buildings or from shipwrecks was re-used, for the second church on St Agnes (now replaced), and the Dining Room floors and wall panelling in the tower at Tresco Abbey. More recently an artist's studio at Bryher used driftwood for its re-construction and iroko from a Seven Stones shipwreck was re-used to build Anneka Rice's new landing quay at Bryher.

The gazetteer in this publication describes numerous buildings on Scilly which have been adapted for new uses, particularly for the provision of tourist accommodation.

Former gigshed at Bryher converted into an Artist's Studio using driftwood

Over the centuries, the islanders, by nature of their isolated situation, developed an ability to master many trades and if necessary change their means of livelihood from farming, fishing and kelping to ship-building, piloting and other industries. The engineering skills in building barrows and fortifications in granite using logs, rollers, levers and man-power have long been admired. Stone was quarried by wetting timber wedges placed in cracks or drilled holes, before the lengthy process of dressing, by hand, to a final size and shape. Despite this, workmanship of the highest order was achieved in the most important buildings, piers and lighthouses.

The quality of joinery and cabinet work was also very high. The Scillonians have been described as natural craftsmen and undoubtedly their expertise arose from the experience they gained in ship building. This is illustrated in the joinery and the skilled carpentry work at Tresco Abbey and St Nicholas Church which were built using local craftsmen.

Timber salvaged from shipwreck re-used for the Dining Room of Tresco Abbey

VERNACULAR ARCHITECTURE

The term vernacular architecture describes the minor buildings of town and countryside, buildings tending to be traditional rather than academic in inspiration.

Cottages at Higher Town, St Martin's, 1822, now re-modelled.

Buildings provided for the simple activities of ordinary people, domestic, agricultural and industrial, related to place, especially through the use of local materials. Although almost totally utilitarian, their simplicity, location, siting and materials have a particular appeal to the twentieth-century visitor.

Most of Scilly's early buildings were either demolished or re-modelled in a programme of improvement during the late 19th century. However, the surviving standing remains of the houses, farm buildings and a gigshed from the late 17th to mid-19th century on the uninhabited island of Samson provide a valuable insight to the vernacular architecture of the islands. Samson was finally evacuated in 1855 and has never been re-occupied, the buildings being left in a ruinous state. As elsewhere on Scilly during this period, the small simple buildings were constructed of granite rubble cleared from the land with some selected or roughly dressed pieces being used for quoins, jambs and lintels. The houses measured between about 15 feet to 25 feet in length by about 12 feet wide. They were either single or two storeys, but invariably low in elevation. Similarly. other non-domestic buildings were small in scale. The roofs of these buildings no longer exist but many of them were probably roofed with a thin layer of thatch held in place by a net of plaited straw and known as rope thatch. The roof pitches were surprisingly low to receive thatch. The structural timbers to the roofs, first floors and internal partitions have also now disappeared as has all the joinery to doors, windows and cupboards. Ground floors were often only swept earth or sand with paving in front of the fireplaces. Windows were generally hornless sashes, usually with sixteen panes although centre-hung casements were also used. Doorways were lower than the height of an average person now and in some cases porches were provided for protection against the elements.

The late 17th century to mid-19th century ruins of one of the cottages on Samson.

Doors to the houses would have been panelled whilst those to farm buildings would have been planked. Window openings were small with internal splays and the majority of the ground floor windows had window-seat ledges. Wall openings were built with granite lintels externally and timber lintels internally. Internal partitions were probably plank and muntin or studwork and lath and plaster. None of the chimneys survived but they were likely to have been constructed in dressed granite or a mixture of rubble and dressed granite.

Elsewhere on Scilly, the buildings have generally been re-modelled or rebuilt. The key characteristics of small scale and construction, with the exception of the thatched roofs, can still be observed. In some cases outshuts have been built to provide additional accommodation at ground floor level.

The small houses, cottages and tenements at Hugh Town, St Mary's are grouped close together, partly as a legacy from early days, when mutual protection against attack was the first essential. The miniature scale of the houses, cottages and farm buildings due to such restricted resources, is also sympathetic to the natural scale of the islands themselves. This characteristic relates to the climatic conditions, with buildings crouching low on sheltered sites, to resist the gales and the spray from the sea. Ceiling heights were often kept low, or buildings restricted to single -storey. The internal ground floor was sometimes kept level with the ground outside or even sunk slightly below ground level. In some cases the use of roof spaces, normally provided with dormer windows, helps to restrict the overall building height. The mass of the buildings is further restricted by the small span of roofs and floors, saving on scarce timber. Hipped or half-hipped roofs were sometimes used to reduce the bulk of the building, and the same small scale was applied to details such as doors, windows and storm porches.

17th-18th century farm building at Higher Town, St Martin's, now used an artist's studio

Huge blocks of granite are used for lower courses with diminishing sizes of granite above. Large corner stones are normally used whilst huge single pieces of granite are employed to provide lintels above door and window openings.

Vernacular architecture on Scilly can still be observed, in the surviving domestic buildings, in the farms, gigsheds and other structures such as the 19th century brewhouse at Bryher. However, they have generally been subject to change of use, alterations or re-modelling.

The Brewhouse, Veronica Farm, Bryher,

ECCLESIASTICAL ARCHITECTURE

Early Christianity on the Isles of Scilly is reflected in the ruins of St Nicholas' Priory, Tresco and the remains of churches and chapels built on the islands during the middle ages, including the church and oratory at St Helen's.

Today, there are six Anglican churches, two methodist churches and a Roman Catholic church. The Church of England is represented by two churches on St Mary's and one on each of the other four inhabited off-islands. The Methodist churches are at St Mary's and St Martin's whilst the Roman Catholic church is located on St Mary's.

The Cornish antiquarian, Dr Borlase, stated in his *Observations on...Scilly* in 1750 that 'all the Churches of the off-islands are built in the same style, from 24 to 32 feet long by 14 feet wide' and that 'they were all built by the family of Godolphin', and I don't think any of them older than the Restoration'.

Since 1750, these off-island Anglican churches have either been subject to alterations and additions, as at the Church of All Saints on Bryher, which now measures 30 feet by 69 feet. Alternatively they have been completely rebuilt, as at St Agnes, (34 feet by 56 feet), St Martin's, (20 feet by 63 feet) and Tresco (48 feet by 81 feet).

The oldest surviving church is at Old Town. The present much loved and beautiful Church is all that remains of the Norman cruciform church c.1130 which was originally built in the form of a cross. Reconstruction of the present

Remains of 12th century church at St Helen's

Sketch by Dr Borlase of typical off-island church, 1750

building began in 1660 and embraces 17th century work including five rectangular windows. The porch and north aisle were built in 1662. A south aisle was added in 1667 and

Norman arch and pillar incorporated into Old Town Church, St Mary's

Interior of the new church at Hugh Town, St Mary's

a gallery was provided for the soldiers from the Garrison. (Supports for this gallery can still be seen at the back). The east end was rebuilt in 1743 but the church had deteriorated so much by the early part of the 19th century it was rebuilt in the 1830s. It was restored in 1890 to its present form when the Reverend W. E. Groves was Chaplain. Subsequently the north-west entrance was added. Overall it now measures 25 feet by 31 feet and represents only part of the previous structure.

There is a round-headed Norman arch and pillar in the north wall adjacent to the vestry - porch.

The new Church of St Mary was built in Hugh Town between 1836 and 1838 by Augustus Smith soon after he became lessee of the islands in 1834. He was educated at Oxford University. Although he had no professional training he acted as amateur architect, quantity surveyor, clerk of works and master builder for the new Church.The building has been described as bold rather than pleasing and plain rather than ornate. In any event it is a strange mixture of styles having a 19th century Gothic-Revival structure, generally embracing pointed lancet arches to external openings, but with exceptions such as the flat-arched door opening to the east side of the tower. Internally, there are further dramatic inconsistencies including the inward facing 'collegiate' style seating and the west gallery.

The Roman Catholic Church in Hugh Town was originally St Mary's school for girls. Built in 1860 as part of Augustus Smith's policy to encourage a high standard of education on the islands, the former first floor classroom is now the chapel of Our Lady - Stella Marie,'Star of the Sea'.

The present Methodist Church on St Mary's, designed by a Scillonian, Alfred Joseph Trenear, was built in 1899 and generally remains unaltered. Externally it is a simple granite structure with a pitched slate roof. The interior is in the form of a horseshoe plan with first floor galleries supported on cast iron columns. Angled stairs lead up to the panel-fronted galleries.

Some of the furnishings originated from the former Georgian Weslyan Methodist chapel in Garrison Lane which was built in 1826. The building is now disused but conversions are being planned to accommodate new uses in the future. The original Wesleyan Chapel on St Mary's was built about 1790 and replaced by a new one on the old site. There was also a further chapel built at Holy Vale on St Mary's in 1862 which was converted for residential use in 1992.

The other existing Methodist church at St, Martin's, built in 1845, overlooks Higher Town Bay. It is a very simple two-cell structure with hipped roofs and plain rendered granite walls. The small interior is interesting with its tiny gallery, brass light fittings and painted woodwork.

Interior of Methodist Church, Church Street, Hugh Town, St Mary's.

MARITIME BUILDINGS

Buildings closely associated with the sea include lighthouses, lighthouse keeper's and coastguard dwellings, lifeboat houses and gig sheds.Lighthouses are often fascinating, majestic and distinctive, and in some cases great feats of engineering. They can be both graceful and stately towers of delicate proportions, yet convey the strength which they need to combat their extreme climatic conditions. They were designed by engineers, architects and builders and today they are a tribute to the skill, determination and legendary courage of the people involved in their construction. Trinity House lighthouse authority is responsible for the major lighthouses on the coast of Cornwall and the Isles of Scilly. They are classified by Trinity House under two main headings, 'land lights' and 'rock lights. The latter group is then sub-divided into 'island lights' and 'pillar lights' which are those built on isolated rocks. Separate dwellings are normally provided for the lighthouse keepers attached to land lights whilst the keepers on rock towers were required to be on continuous duty and live in the accommodation provided within or adjacent to the lighthouses themselves. The lights from seven lighthouses are visible from the Isles of Scilly, namely, Lizard, Pendeen, Longships, Wolf, Peninnis, Round Island and the Bishop. Pendeen and Lizard stand on the mainland and Longships is built on a reef of granite just over a mile off Lands End, whilst

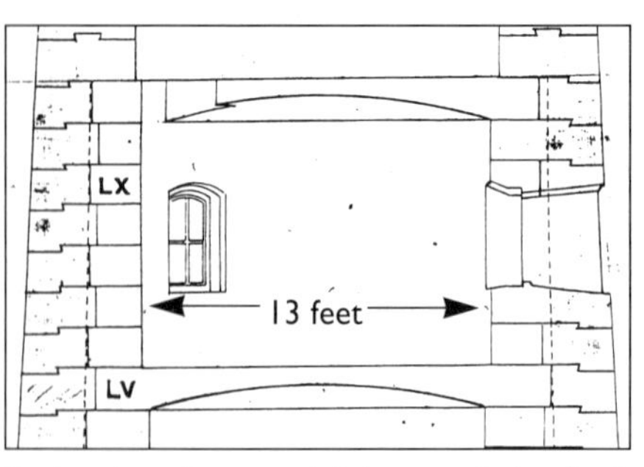

Section through existing lighthouse at Bishop Rock showing outer granite casing.

Bedroom to Bishop Rock lighthouse showing survuving curved bunk beds.

Wolf is about midway between Penzance and Scilly. The remaining three lighthouses form an inner ring of lights around the Isles of Scilly. The one at Peninnis is a steel trestle tower built in 1911 on the southern point of St Mary's. This lighthouse replaced the one at St Agnes which is now disused, although still regarded as a daymark. St Agnes lighthouse is important historically since it is one of earliest to be built in the U.K. and originally it was lit every night by means of a coal fire. It was described in the 18th century by Dr Borlase, to be 'the greatest ornament of this Island' and 'a fine Column' standing on the highest ground at St Agnes. However, although it is a striking and attractive landmark, its form, like other lighthouses, followed its function as a navigational aid and a warning to shipping of hazardous conditions. The importance of St Agnes had been reduced to some extent during the 19th century when the well-known lighthouse at Bishop Rock was erected.

The first lighthouse at Bishop Rock was an iron structure which after three years of arduous work and before completion, was completely swept away overnight during a violent storm in 1850. The engineer-in-charge was Nicholas Douglass and between 1852 and 1858, he was responsible for replacing the initial lighthouse

Lighthouse keeper's dwelling at St Agnes

Lifeboat House, St Agnes, rebuilt in 1904

with a massive tower built in granite. Even this new structure was vulnerable in heavy seas and led to it being strengthened with an outer crust of interlocking granite blocks and steel rods. At the same time its height was increased to 167 feet. The engineer-in-charge of the rebuilding was William Tregarthen Douglass and the work was completed in 1882. The granite was obtained from quarries on the mainland due to the high price and non-availability of stone on the islands. The granite was transported to workshops which were built at Rat Island on St Mary's for preparation and working. Subsequently it was transported by special boats to the island of Rosevear, which was the base for the construction team, and then to Bishop Rock itself. The accuracy and workmanship of the dovetailed granite blocks and the fine (approximately 6mm) joints is astonishing, particularly in view of the working conditions. The accommodation, all on different levels in the multi-storey tower, included a living room, a bedroom with curved bunk beds, engine rooms and various stores. In 1977 a steel and aluminium helicopter landing platform was added which received a Structural Steel Design Award.

The use of a helicopter has overcome the difficult problem of servicing and maintaining this lighthouse and the one at Round Island by boats.Their recent automation has meant that resident keepers are no longer necessary. Both the lighthouses at Round Island and St Agnes were provided with separate dwellings for the keepers. The former one is a simple flat-roofed single-storey structure whilst the house at St Agnes, now a private dwelling, is far more elaborate with a steeply pitched slate roof. There is also a row of coastguard houses overlooking the coast on the southern side of St Agnes. Two pairs of houses were provided for lighthouse keepers on the Garrison at St Mary's which are similar to other such houses found on the mainland. These dwellings are painted white as are all of the lighthouses at Scilly, with the exception of the one at Bishop Rock which is built in fairfaced granite. There are no lighthouses on St Martin's, but there is a very early example of a daymark in the form of a cylinder surmounted by a cone. It was erected on the north-eastern tip of St Martin's in 1683 by Thomas Ekins. The hollow granite structure is rendered and distinguished by its red and white striped painted finish.

Lifeboat houses were built at St Mary's and St Agnes The one at Periglis on St Agnes was rebuilt in 1904 with a special launch-way and rails to accommodate a trolley for the lifeboat. Gigsheds also survive on various islands.

Gigshed, Bryher, converted into an Artist's Studio

Harry's Walls, an unfinished fort on St Mary's

The fortifications on Scilly and their associated buildings are important both historically and architecturally. Not only are these buildings and fortifications well preserved, the construction of their granite walls is remarkable for its magnitude, skill and craftsmanship. Following the decline of Ennor Castle at Old Town on St Mary's there was an abortive attempt in about 1550 to replace it with the badly sited fort known as Harry's Walls to the north-west of Hugh Town. Other military buildings erected between 1548 and 1554 included King Charles Castle,two blockhouses on Tresco and a third on the north-east coast of St Mary's. In 1593, Queen Elisabeth instructed Sir Francis Godolphin to build the principal new fort, namely Star Castle, as protection against Spain, pirates and privateers. The site selected was the high rocky peninsula which was joined to the main part of St Mary's by the sand bar now occupied by Hugh Town. The work was carried out in an extremely short space of time between January 1593 and December 1594 with advice from Robert Adams, an engineer and England's coastal defence expert. The building was erected very quickly and designed with elegant proportions. The site supervision and cost control were also commended in a letter from Sir Francis Godolphin to Lord Burghley dated 6th August 1593. 'Adams is well deserving, for besides his perfect skill in numbers and measures, he is very provident in saving, and no less painful in attending, the work considered, so much has seldom been performed at such small charge and with so few hands in so short a time'. Sir Francis Godolphin also admired the design of the Castle for having '... so tempered strength with delight' and being '... as it serveth for a sure Hold and Commodious Dwelling'. The Castle which is a fort, governor's residence and prison derives its name from its plan in the shape of an eight-pointed star. The castle's two-storey residence and its basement were originally built inside a moat and had a thatched roof. It is surrounded by an eighteen-foot high granite curtain wall surmounted by ramparts with numerous embrasures for cannons and muskets. Four small rooms on the ramparts were provided for the captains of the garrison. The bellcote over the entrance was added in the 18th century.

Upon completion of Star Castle, Godolphin began fortifying the east side of the peninsula or Hugh by building the first section of the curtain wall and its batteries. Other ancillary buildings built in the late 16th century included the Garrison Windmill Tower, Rocket House magazine and the adjoining prison. During the Spanish Wars between 1715 and 1750, the

Entrance to Star Castle at the Garrison, St Mary's

neglected Garrison was transformed under Master Gunner Abraham Tovey when the walls were extended around the perimeter with the exception of the north-west coast.
A group of imposing ashlar faced buildings were added at this time to provide accommodation, workshops and stores. In 1742, Tovey rebuilt the Garrison Gateway, an earlier Elisabethan structure, and added the bell-tower.
Another new fort, namely Cromwell's Castle was built in 1651 as a defence against the Dutch. It was sited at sea level on the west coast of Tresco. Stone for the building was obtained from the ruins of King Charles Castle standing on the promontory above. The building is a tall tower, circular on plan. There is an open gun platform to the roof of the ribbed stone vault which spans the main room below. A further gun platform was added to the seaward side of the tower by Abraham Tovey c.1740.

Sally Port to Rocket House at the Garrison, St Mary's

19th and 20th CENTURY ARCHITECTURE

The increased prosperity of the Scillonians since the beginning of the 19th century was due to the development of profit-making industries such as ship-building, exporting flowers and the growth in tourism. This increase in affluence brought about the re-development and expansion of Hugh Town as well as a general improvement in the buildings throughout the islands. Hugh town is partly situated on a low sandy peninsula which connects St Mary's to the Garrison on the hill, formerly known as the Hugh. It has one principal street, a pleasant central space and many narrow and irregular runaways to the water's edge.
Between 1800 and 1820 admirable simple well-built terraces of two- and three-storey houses were built in Hugh Town. They extend along the south side of the Park, the central open space on the sand bar, and then follow the line of the south side of Church street. Their granite walls are either left natural or rendered and limewashed. The masonry is worked with extreme care and attention to detail is reflected in the bay and bow windows, lattice porches, panelled doors and fanlights.
At this time a few individual houses were built which were larger than their neighbours. For example, Lemon Hall in Church Street and Lyonesse in the Strand with their carefully proportioned and rendered Regency facades. These both illustrate the growing influence from the mainland and assume an unusual importance as does the Custom House in the Strand, a former stuccoed house with its decorative external staircase balustrade and porch.
After taking up a new 99 year lease of Scilly from the Duchy of Cornwall in 1834, the new

self-styled 'Lord Proprietor' Augustus Smith was required under the terms and conditions of the lease to provide a new church and to extend the pier on St.Mary's. These building projects were completed in 1838 although the pier was later extended again in 1889 and further improved in 1994. Whilst the new church was being constructed, Smith built his own residence, namely Tresco Abbey, and created the surrounding famous gardens Subsequently this granite building was substantially enlarged by a number of extensions. The rough granite walls of the Abbey have been described as having 'just enough workmanship to prevent its looking commonplace but not enough to give it that cold, formal workhouse looking appearance ...' In 1860, Smith also built the Valhalla open-air museum in Tresco Gardens which was to be extended in 1958 using the same matching materials, unusual construction and playful details.

Detail of porch to terrace houses South side of the Parade, Hugh Town 1810

During the mid-19th century Augustus Smith constructed new schools on all the main islands and in effect, made education compulsory. A girls' school was built on the Strand in 1860 (the present Roman Catholic Church), a boys' school at Carn Thomas (the present public library and infants' department) and an infants' school in Church Street (the present Church Hall). Not only was Smith responsible for ensuring a very high standard of education on Scilly, he also provided good vocational training in which navigation figured prominently. Furthermore, he supported the rise in the ship-building industry at Scilly during the 19th century. Several Anglican churches were provided at this time as well as the Bishop Rock lighthouse and Trinity House Cottages for the keepers. Towards the end of the 19th century, Round Island lighthouse was built (1887) and several prominent buildings of architectural interest were erected in Hugh Town. These included the Town Hall (1889), the Post Office (1897) and the new Methodist Church in Church Street (1899) which replaced the previous one built in Garrison Lane.

The 20th century heralded a further phase in building and development on Scilly particularly on St Mary's. In 1926 the Duchy of Cornwall replaced houses, cottages and Mumford's shop either side of Hugh Street with new flat-roofed terrace houses. These are carefully built and

Eaves detail to Valhalla

Terrace Houses at Parsons Field, Hugh Town, St Mary's

Helipad, Bishop Rock Lighthouse, Structural Steel Award 1977

well-detailed in granite and add to the pleasing severity and neatness of Hugh Street. Other similar contemporary terrace houses in granite with flat roofs were built by the Duchy in rural areas at Porthloo and Longstone on St Mary's. By the 1930s other buildings had been provided in the town, including Barclays Bank with its colourwashed and rendered granite facade, and the Isles of Scilly Steamship Company's offices. In the mid 19th century Lloyds Bank was built in Hugh Street with its symmetrical colourwashed rendered facade built in granite rubble with a classical porch supported on Roman Doric columns. In 1951 a row of two-storey local authority houses with porches were built along the north side of Parsons Field The architects were Bazeley and Barbary. Their walls were constructed of rendered concrete blocks. Delabole roof slates were specified, although unfortunately these have been replaced with cement slates.

During the 1960s a further Duchy of Cornwall Housing Scheme was built in Launceston Close at Old Town. Designed by architects Louis de Soissons, well-known for their housing associated with the Welwyn Garden City movement. Also at that time the new Secondary School was built at Carn Thomas together with the new Museum in Church Street.

Buildings erected in the 1970s included the new Airport Terminal Building which was extended in 1994, a terraced housing project between Silver Street and Parsons Field by architect T. J. Hiron and a new Primary School near Old Town. With the increase in tourism, new hotels have been provided such as the Island Hotel at Tresco and St Martin's Hotel, built in 1962 and 1987-89 respectively.

During the 1990s there have been further building conversions on Scilly including the use of a barn at St Mary's to form a restaurant at Seaways Farm (1993) and a shop and public house at Old Town (1994-95).

Interior of Airport Terminal Building St Mary's

St Martin's Hotel

GAZETTEER

This gazetteer contains examples of Scillonian architecture from all periods. Many of them are Listed under the 1990 Planning Act as being of special architectural or historic interest (Grades I, II, and II*). Those in the first division include Star Castle and the Rocket House. Ten ancient monuments have been placed in the guardianship of the State by the Duchy of Cornwall including five prehistoric burial chambers and five fortifications namely, the Rocket House and Garrison walls, Harry's Walls, King Charles's Castle, Cromwell Castle and the Old Blockhouse on Tresco.

The inhabited islands are each treated separately and the buildings are numbered in a clockwise direction on the outline maps at the beginning of each individual section. The buildings in Hugh Town, St Mary's are numbered on the separate street map included in the centre pages. It is important to note that although the majority of the examples described can be seen from the public highway or public footpaths, they are often in private ownership and inaccessible to the public. This note applies to many of the farmhouses, residential buildings and lighthouses although churches and the fortifications are generally open to visitors.

TRESCO

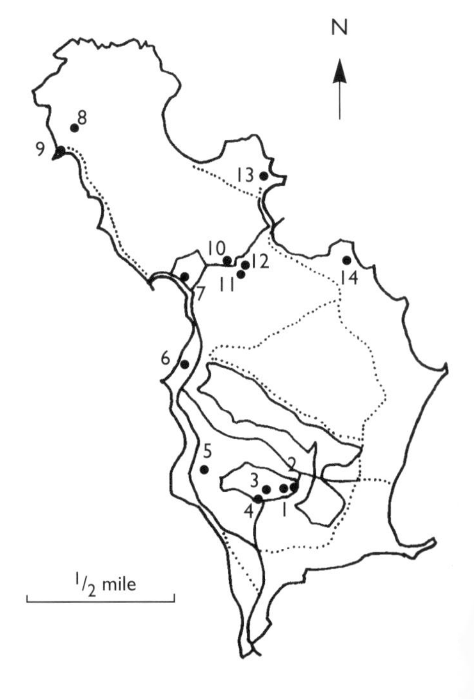

1 TRESCO ABBEY

[SV 895143]

1838-1891. Augustus Smith, first 'Lord Proprietor' of the Isles of Scilly from 1834 to 1872, designed the Abbey to provide a new home for himself. The house was habitable by 1838 and was initially completed in 1843. A complex plan evolved by various extensions in 1861, and the addition of a dominant square tower at the east end in 1891. The tower was designed by Smith's nephew, Thomas Algernon Dorrien-Smith Today, the composition of the Abbey reflects its phased development. The use of local roughly coursed granite with ashlar dressings and slate roofs throughout helps to unify the design and relate it to its unique site. Principal rooms include the Dining Room, Library, Drawing Room, Study, Long Gallery and Billiard Room. Floorboards in the Dining Room and wall panelling to the Billiard Room in the Tower make use of timbers salvaged from wrecked ships. Some of the granite used for the building was obtained from the promontory on which it stands and much of the work was carried out by local masons. Augustus Smith also designed the superb surrounding gardens which are open to visitors, although the Abbey itself and its own grounds are private.

2 GATEHOUSE TO TRESCO ABBEY

[SV 895143]

1843. A picturesque Gothic-revival style building by Augustus Smith situated at the south-east end of Abbey Road built with roughly coursed granite rubble walls and slate roofs. The two-storey building appears to grow out of the huge adjacent granite rubble wall between the gatehouse and the Abbey itself. The upper floor bridges the gateway with its pitched roof meeting a distinctive two-storey tower surmounted by a pyramidal roof.

3 TRESCO PRIORY

[SV 895143]

c.1300. The attractive remains of the Priory form an integral part of Tresco Gardens. Still surviving, although subject to substantial rebuilding in the 19th century, are some granite walls of the nave of a 13th century church and two pointed arches.

4 VALHALLA

[SV 893142]

c.1860 This open air museum in the corner of Tresco Gardens was founded by Augustus Smith to display his collection of figureheads, stern boards and other parts of ships wrecked on the islands. It was named after Valhalla, the mythological Norse palace in which the souls of dead heroes feast. A matching extension was provided in 1958 at ninety degrees to the original building. The materials, construction and details are playful and a delight. The pantile covered roofs are supported on piers formed with large boulders of granite balanced precariously on top of each other. A slate plaque commemorates both Augustus Smith and the restoration work carried out by Thomas Dorrien-Smith. The collection is now owned and maintained by the National Maritime Museum.

5 SMITH MONUMENT

[SV 891143]

1872. Designed by Augustus Smith himself. Although he was buried at St Buryan in Cornwall, his official memorial is this rough-hewn granite monument which is built of rocks from the sea, and stands on the south side of Abbey Hill, Tresco overlooking the islands.

6 MILL

[SV 889149]

c. 1835. Designed by Augustus Smith, this building was originally used as a barley mill and for smoking fish. It has now been converted into holiday accommodation. The machinery has been retained in the exposed roof space of the two-storey section of the building. The walls and the circular chimney are built in granite and the roofs are covered with slates. An underground passage, believed to still be in existence, led from the mill down to the Great Pool.

7 COTTAGES, NEW GRIMSBY

[SV 889153]

Late 18th - early 19th century. Situated along the west shoreline, these picturesque cottages reflect their exposed positions with their low elevations, small window openings and storm-porches. Although the terraces of cottages are all built in granite, their appearance is varied by the use of fairface granite or rendered finishes and in some cases the application of whitewash. The porches to one row of cottages are built with large blocks of unwrought granite. In some instances the natural slate roofs and small timber windows have been retained. However, there has been an

unfortunate tendency for replacement cement slates and plastic windows to be introduced which lack the weathering characteristics of natural materials.

8 KING CHARLES' CASTLE

[SV 882161]

1550-54. Built on the summit of Castle Hill at the north end of Tresco, this fort was badly sited and had a short active life since it guns could not fire downwards into the Channel. It now lies in ruins but it was originally divided into two parts with the armament amassed on the western side to cover the entrance to New Grimsby harbour, and the domestic quarters for the garrison behind to the east. The western end is semi-hexagonal to provide a wide field of fire, and was originally two-storied to give at least two tiers of guns. The domestic quarters are in the form of a main room which served as a hall with a large fireplace and a kitchen containing another fireplace and a well-built oven on one side. Doors led into small chambers, probably sleeping quarters, and beyond the main entrance is the guardroom.

9 CROMWELL'S CASTLE

[SV 882160]

1651-52 This gun tower, with its 12 feet thick walls is built of randomly coursed granite rubble, similar in style to the outer walls of Star Castle on St Mary's. It is 150 feet in circumference and 60 feet high and stands about 20 feet above the water level overlooking Tresco Channel, almost directly below King Charles's Castle, which it replaced. The tower was originally entered through a doorway at high level on the south side with a stair leading down to the first floor living room and an unlighted basement below. There is evidence from existing beam and joist holes, midway between the floor and vault, that at one time there was another intermediate floor. The stair in the wall leads up to a gun platform over the stone vault. The platform is open to the sky and six gunports are contained in the thickness of the wall. A seaward facing gun platform was constructed c.1740. The present entrance to the tower was formed by Master Gunner Abraham Tovey who was responsible for the building works at the Garrison on St Mary's. (For floor plans of nos 8 and 9 see 'Ancient Monuments of the Isles of Scilly' published by HMSO)

10 HOUSES, DOLPHIN TOWN

[SV 892154]

Early and mid 19th century. Two houses defining the road opposite the church. Built with whitewashed granite rubble and stepped slate roofs. Outshuts project to the rear of the houses and chimney stacks. are formed in granite and brickwork.

11 COTTAGES, DOLPHIN TOWN

[SV 892154]

Early 19th century. Individual picturesque cottages adjacent to the church built with whitewashed granite rubble and 20th century slate roofs includes one known as 'Thatch', which until 1989-90 was the last cottage on the islands to have retained its thatched roof.

12 CHURCH OF ST NICHOLAS

[SV 892154]

1878-79. Until 1798 the church at Tresco consisted of two cottages which formed an aisle and a south transept. The present building was designed by Thomas Algernon Dorrien-Smith in memory of his uncle, Augustus Smith and was funded by Lady Sophia Tower. The builders are recognised from the inscriptions in the porch; 'built by Richard and Thomas Chudleigh, masons and William Nicholls, carpenter.' The church was opened in 1879 by the first Bishop of Truro, Dr

St Nicholas Church, Tresco

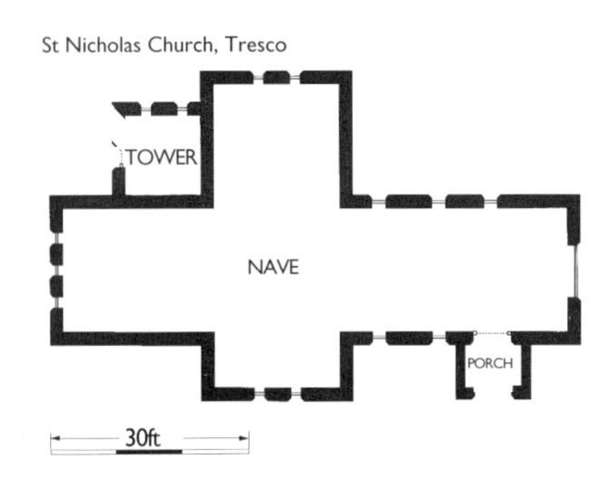

Edward Benson, and later consecrated and dedicated by the succeeding Bishop, Dr Wilkinson. St Nicholas is the patron saint of sailors, children, travellers, merchants and those in distress. The organ was installed in 1886. The church, based upon a cruciform plan, comprises a chancel, nave transepts, north porch and the unusual feature of a south-east tower. The open arch-braced roof is set on stone corbels and the difficult problem of spanning the transepts was solved by the head carpenter who suggested basing it upon an upturned boat. Decorative encaustic tiles are used for the floor of the sanctuary. The stained glass windows by the young artist C. E. Kempe include designs for the three east lancet windows and the west rose window, whilst the one to the north transept is by W. E. Tower, a pupil and partner of Kempe. A memorial plaque on the north wall of the chancel, designed by the Hon. Claud Phillimore, commemorates five Dorrien-Smith sons who died in World War II.

13 **ISLAND HOTEL**

[SV 893159]

1962. Designed by John Strubbe, architect, the building is discreetly sited on the east coast of Tresco overlooking Old Grimsby harbour and incorporated an older existing building. Materials include imported western red cedar cladding.

14 **OLD BLOCKHOUSE**

[SV 897155]

c. 1548-52. Built entirely of granite on an elevated site overlooking St Helen's Pool and the harbour of Old Grimsby, this defence outpost consists of a rectangular platform paved with stone and approached by stone steps from the west. At one

time it had a parapet with embrasures at least to the western ends of the northern and southern sides of the building. The living quarters were meagre but a further room with two small windows and a fireplace were added to the south-west corner at a later date. In the Parliamentary Survey of 1652 it was known as Dover Fort.

15 **ROUND ISLAND LIGHTHOUSE**

[SV 902177]

1887. Although only 46 feet high up to the lantern gallery, the lighthouse is built in a commanding position on top of Round Island, 180 feet above sea level. It was constructed by the engineer-in-charge William Tregarthen Douglass. Circular on plan, the tapering three stage tower is built with granite ashlar painted white culminating in a curved conical roof and lattice light. The light source itself was modernised in 1967. The attached single-storey house is built with a flat roof and projecting cornice. Relief supplies from boats were provided by means of an aerial hoist but it was removed during the 1970s following automation and access by helicopter.

ST MARTIN'S

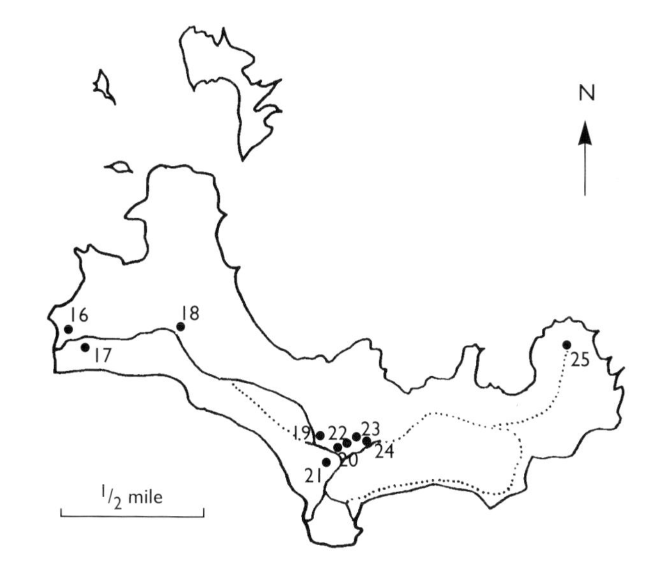

15

16 ST MARTIN'S HOTEL

[SV 915162]

1989. The hotel is one of the newest buildings on the Isles of Scilly. The use of forms, scale and some traditional materials which partially reflect Scilly's vernacular architecture help to reduce its impact on the site, which could be described as inoffensive. The hotel, is situated on the western tip of the island facing the seashore. Inevitably however it intrudes on its exceptionally beautiful and peaceful surroundings although its design aims to mitigate this problem. However, it raises questions about the choice of site and the lost opportunity to produce an outstanding and progressive architectural solution. Ironically, the use of granite taken from stone hedges on the island raised objections from environmental conservationists.

17 ASHVALE FARM, LOWER TOWN

[SV 916161]

Mid 19th century. An older former dwelling has been incorporated into this farmhouse when it was extended to form an L-shaped plan, the older section forming the west wing. Built in uncoursed and roughly coursed granite rubble, the building harmonises with its surroundings. The original roof coverings have been replaced by slates and red pantiles.Red brick and granite chimney stacks are provided at either end of the 19th century extension and there is a further truncated brick stack to the older section of the building.

18 BARN AT MIDDLE TOWN

[SV 921162]

19th century. Typical of the farm outbuildings from this period found on Scilly with roughly coursed granite rubble walls and gabled pantile roof. The flush verges with their rough mortar cappings is a typical detail found throughout the islands.

19 CHURCH OF ST MARTIN

[SV 929156]

Rebuilt 1867-68. Situated at high level in a very exposed position but with spectacular views, St Martin's Church is believed to have been built on the site of an 11th/12th century chapel and graveyard. The slate roof and window cills have unfortunately been replaced during the 20th century with artificial slates. The original building, erected in 1683 by Thomas Ekin, the Godolphin Steward, was initially very small extending to only 20 feet in length. Subsequently it was enlarged and then repaired by the Reverend George Woodley in 1821. Following damage by lightning in 1866 the church was rebuilt by Augustus Smith. The AS monogram can be seen on the

St. Martin's Church

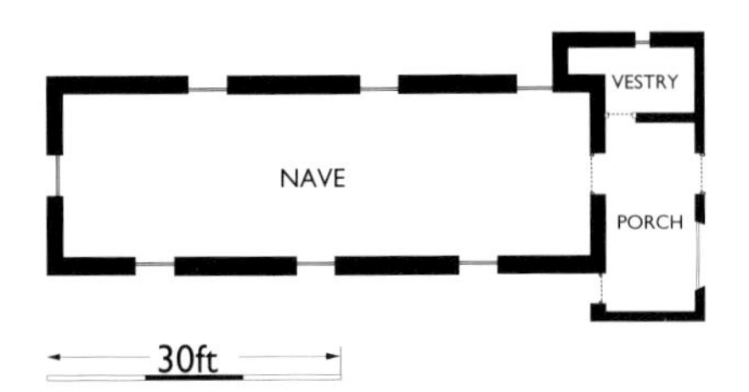

bell turret. The East window by Clayton and Bell depicts St Martin and the Beggar. There is a small timber gallery to the west end. The floor to the sanctuary is covered with decorative encaustic tiles whilst stone flagstones are used for the central aisle of the nave. A block of granite built into the east wall is thought to be a medieval cross base whilst the pillar in the churchyard may have been the base of an ancient sundial.

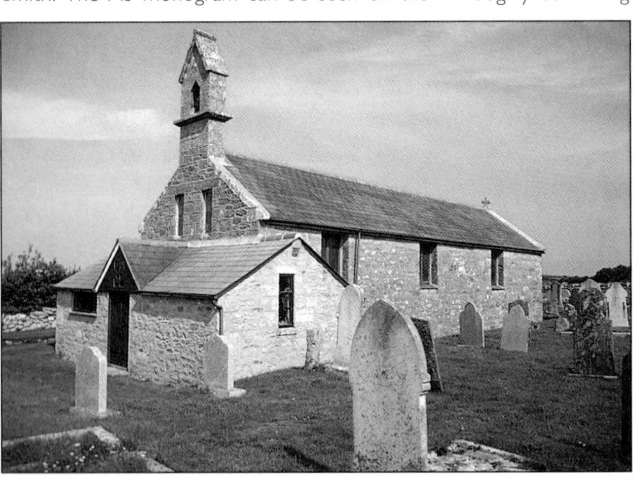

20 HOUSE AT HIGHER TOWN

[SV 929156]

Early - mid 19th century. Detached house built in roughly coursed granite, partially rendered and painted white. There is a rear outshut to the left hand side of the house and it has recently been extended at the rear. The gabled roof with its stone ridge has been re-covered with artificial slates. The granite chimney stacks are constructed with drip courses.

21 METHODIST CHURCH, ROCK, HIGHER TOWN

[SV 929155]

1845. A simple chapel with a secondary room which steps down the hillside. The granite rubble walls are finished with natural stucco blocked out as ashlar. Pitched and hipped roofs are covered with slates. Internally there is a panel fronted gallery which is supported on cast-iron columns with moulded capitals.

22 FARM BUILDINGS, HIGHER TOWN

[SV 930156]

17th-18th century. A series of buildings which at one time formed part of North Farm including a cowhouse, pigsty, various outbuildings and a stable which has now been converted into an artist's gallery and studio. All built in roughly coursed granite rubble with red pantile and artificial slate roofs. This group of buildings exemplify the types found on Scillonian farms.

23 NORTH FARM, HIGHER TOWN

[SV 930156]

17th-18th century. Farmhouse constructed in roughly coursed granite with a hipped slate roof, this two-storey building was remodelled in the 19th century.

24 COTTAGES, HIGHER TOWN

[SV 930155]

Late 18th-mid 19th century. Cottages at the east end of Higher Town include a row of three cottages with roughly coursed granite rubble walls and 20th century slate roofs Adjacent to the Methodist Church at Rock two cottages, with the date 1822 inscribed in it a granite lintel over the front door, have been remodelled and extended in the late 19th century to provide a single dwelling. Stepping down to roadside from Rock are a number of interesting small cottages with rendered wall finishes and tiny porches.

25 DAYMARK

[SV 942161]

1683. Erected by Thomas Ekins, the first steward of the Godolphin family. This 16 feet diameter circular rendered granite hollow tower, with internal steps, is about 40 feet high. It is the earliest surviving dated example of a beacon in the British Isles. The date of 1637 above the sealed entrance is incorrect. Painted white until 1822, red in 1833, and now in red and white bands.

Hugh Town, St Mary's

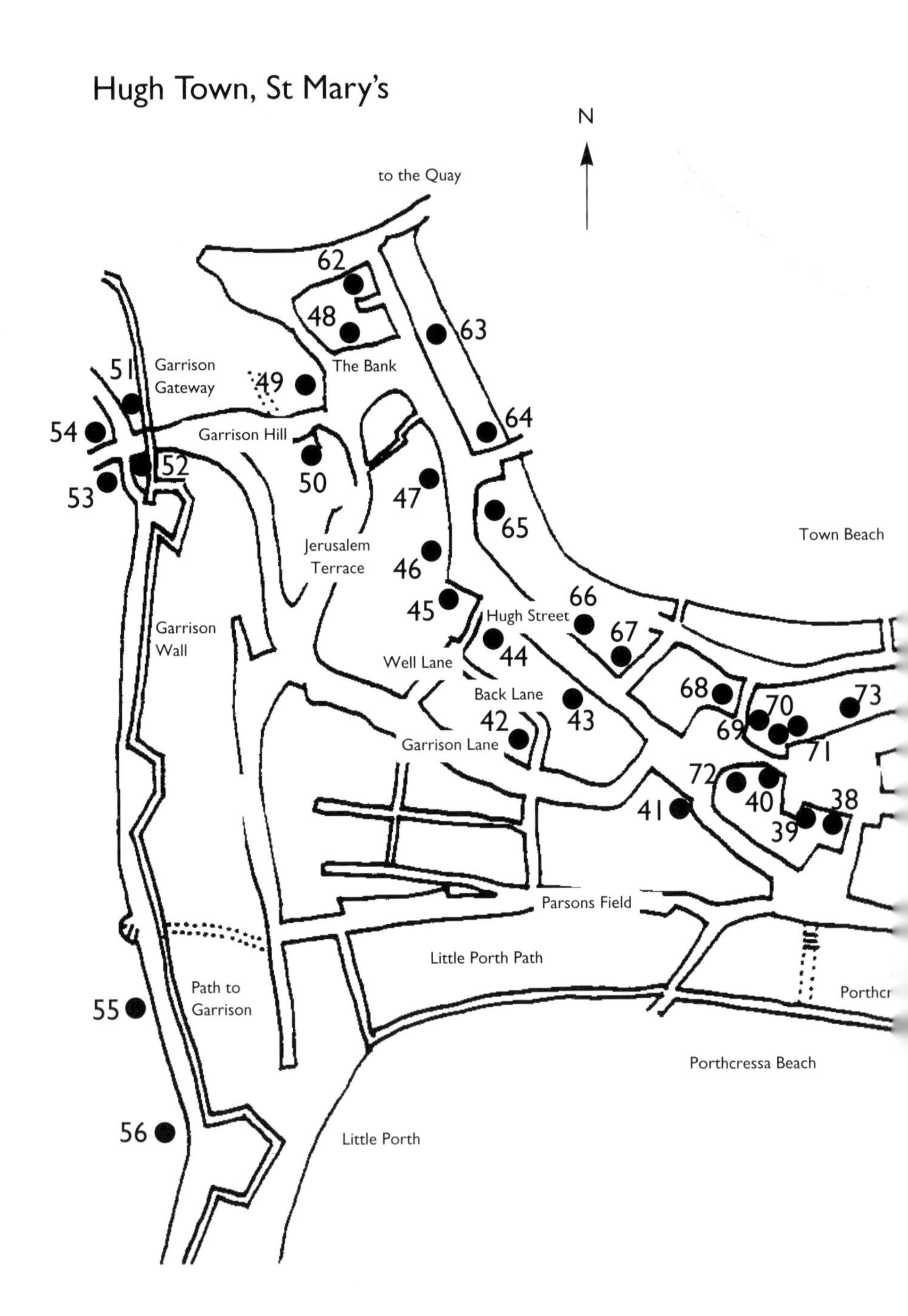

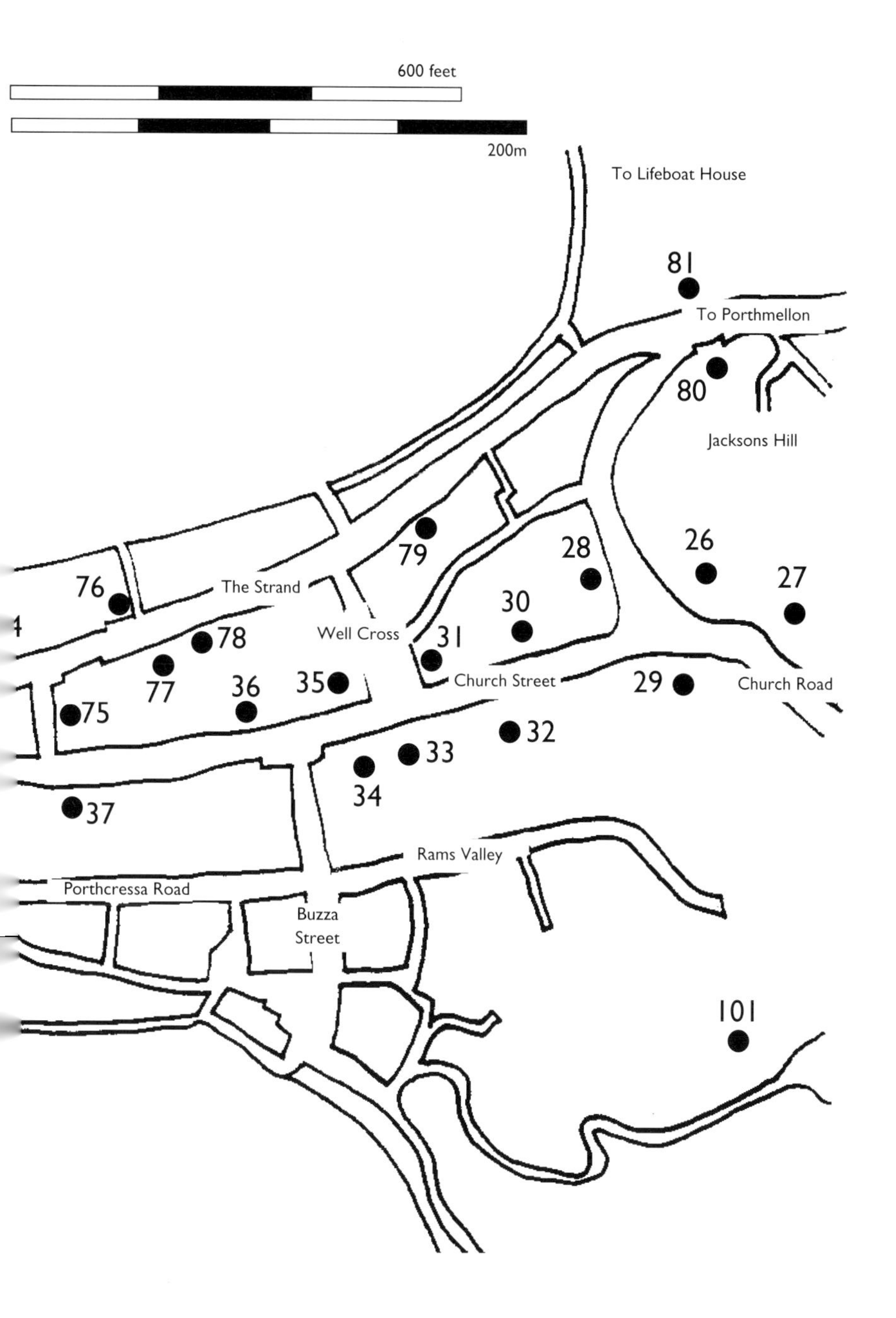

600 feet
200m
To Lifeboat House
81
To Porthmellon
80
Jacksons Hill
79
28
26
27
76
The Strand
30
Well Cross
31
78
77
36
35
Church Street
29
Church Road
75
32
33
34
37
Rams Valley
Porthcressa Road
Buzza
Street
101

ST MARY'S

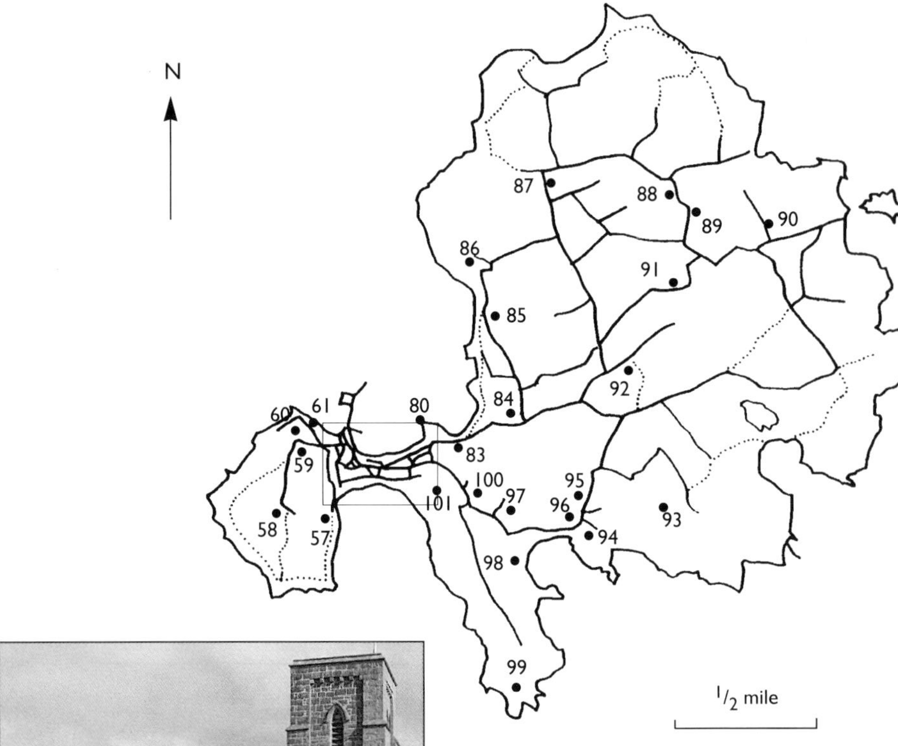

St. Mary's Church

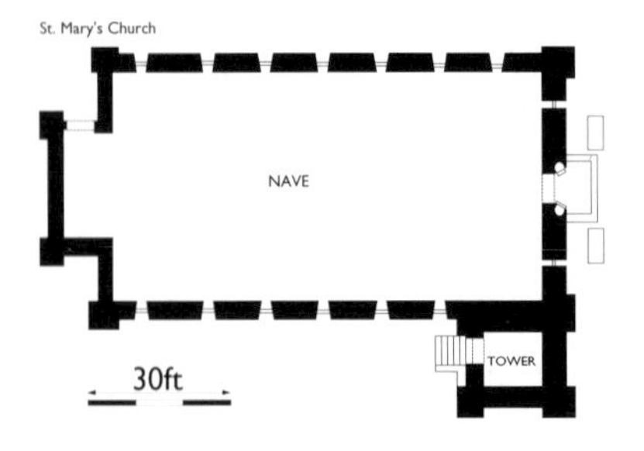

26 PARISH CHURCH OF ST MARY THE VIRGIN

[SV 906106]

The main church of the islands with its beautiful stained glass was built between 1836 and 1838 and consecrated by the Bishop of Exeter in 1838.

27 THE CHAPLAINCY

[SV 907105]

c.1830. A simple elegant detached two-storey house with a pilastered porch and sash windows

which may have evolved from two smaller dwellings. Rendered granite rubble painted white with hipped slate roofs. Internal features include well-proportioned rooms, a finely detailed open-well staircase which sweeps up to a large landing. There is a Greek-style cornice to one of the first floor rooms.

28 GODOLPHIN HOTEL, CHURCH STREET

[SV 906106]

1939. Originally named St Mary's Hall and built as a residence for an Italian nobleman, Count Leon Ferrari who married a Scillonian. The original two-storey building makes use of local granite and features a sturdy low tower. The rear and side extensions were added at a later date.

29 FIELD HOUSE, CHURCH STREET

[SV 906105]

19th century. An imposing two-storey detached house which has been converted into flats. Bay windows are provided at ground floor level whilst dormer windows serve the roof space. Painted render to granite walls with plain corner pilasters and slate roofs.

30 TERRACE HOUSES, NORTH SIDE, CHURCH STREET

[SV 906106]

19th century. An attractive row of two-storey houses with bay windows to ground and first floors. Dormer windows with curved heads to sash windows serve the rooms in the roof spaces. Built with coursed granite walls and slate roofs, the houses have been converted into apartments.

31 METHODIST CHURCH

[SV 906106]

1899. Designed by a Scillonian, Alfred Joseph Trenear the Church has remained unaltered since it was built. A simple granite structure with a pitched slate roof. The interior is in the form of a horseshoe plan with first floor galleries supported on cast iron columns.

32 TERRACE HOUSES, SOUTH SIDE, CHURCH STREET

[SV 905105]

19th century. Two and three-storey terraced houses generally with roof spaces lit by dormer windows. Dwarf front garden walls in coursed and dressed granite with spear-headed railings. The houses are interrupted by the Hotel, a cottage, and a pair of semi-detached houses dating from c.1840. The three-storey houses date from the early 19th century and are built in rendered granite rubble with a concave-chamfered granite eaves cornice. Normally rectangular sash windows are used although exceptions include curved heads to some dormer windows and a canted oriel window with sashes. In one case a bay window extends up from the ground level to first floor. The houses further to the west include interesting details such as semi-circular arches with voussoirs and granite lintels over door and window openings.

33 BELL ROCK HOTEL, CHURCH STREET

[SV 905105]

Early-mid 19th century with 20th century additions. A two-storey building with attics which was originally built as a house but subsequently converted into a hotel. A second storey was added to the single storey west wing in the 20th century Hipped dormer windows are also 20th century. Materials used include granite rubble with aggregate render and tiled roof.

34 COTTAGE ADJOINING BELL ROCK HOTEL, CHURCH STREET

[SV 905105]

Early 19th century. Two-storey building. White painted granite rubble walls with quoins and a slate roof. Rear 1980s extension. Coursed and dressed granite walls define the front garden. 19th century Scillonian interior features have been retained such as panelled shutters and doors, moulded joinery and wood bressummer over an open fireplace.

35 LEMON HALL, NORTH SIDE, CHURCH STREET

[SV 905106]

c.1820-1830. Two-storey Regency house with sash windows and doorway with pilasters. Constructed in granite with painted render externally and slate roof behind parapet walls and eaves cornices. Single -storey rear wing with hipped roofs. Fine cantilevered open-well staircase to the rear of the hallway.

36 MUSEUM

[SV 904106]

1967.Designed by architect Geoffrey Drewitt. Some traditional materials such as exposed granite and render have been incorporated to relate the building to its context but influenced by the clean uncluttered lines aspired to by the 20th century modern movement in architecture. The interior is more interesting with its spatial interplay between the semi-basement and the upper ground floor. The first and second floors contain flats with cantilevered concrete balconies.There is a fascinating collection of exhibits.

37 TERRACE HOUSES, SOUTH SIDE, THE PARADE

[SV 904105]

Early 19th century. A row of four two-storey houses with attics, linked to the adjacent five two-storey houses in Church Street of a similar or slightly later period. Built in either

exposed roughly coursed and squared granite or coursed granite rubble except in one case where pebbledash render has been used to the front elevation. Roofs and cheeks to hipped dormers are covered with slates. Interesting individual features include slightly bowed and canted bay windows, metal trellis work to porches, and the use of granite lintels and semi-circular arches with granite voussoirs over external wall openings.

38 HOUSE ADJOINING TOWN HALL, THE PARADE

[SV 903105]

Late 18th-early 19th century. Two-storey house built in coursed granite rubble with some squared stone to the front elevation, all painted white. Slate covered roof and rendered chimney. Exceptionally good example of a complete 19th century Scillonian interior with panelled doors, muntin partitions to central stair and 20th century outshut to rear. Adjacent rear single-storey outbuilding of a similar period built with coursed granite rubble, gabled pantile roof and brick chimney stack.

39 **TOWN HALL, THE PARADE**

[SV 903105]

1889. Designed by architect J. Goodfellow, the Town Hall is multi-functional serving as a public hall and theatre, local authority offices, Council Chambers and Magistrates' Court. Rectangular on plan and two storeys high its classical style is reflected in its pedimented front, symmetrical window pattern, plinth, angle quoins and keyed four-centred arches over openings. Materials used include squared and roughly coursed and snecked granite with hammer dressed details and stone copings to the gabled roof. The interior has been subject to alterations.

40 **PAIR OF HOUSES, SOUTH SIDE, THE PARADE**

[SV 903105]

Early 19th century. Two-storey houses with attics. Now used for holiday apartments. Built in roughly coursed granite and M-shaped and half-hipped slate covered roofs. Semi-circular arches to doorways with voussoirs. Half-hipped dormers with slate-hung cheeks and rendered ridge chimney stacks.

41 **BISHOP AND WOLF PUBLIC HOUSE, SILVER STREET**

[SV 902105]

c. 1700. Formerly a house built for Thomas Ekins, first land agent for the Godolphin Estate, resident on the Islands from 1683 and responsible for the erection of the daymark on St Martin's. A two-storey building with attics which is particularly

valuable both historically and architecturally, as one of the earliest surviving houses on Scilly. Constructed in coursed granite rubble with dressed and coursed granite to the front elevation, slate roof and granite chimney stacks. Hipped roof dormers have vertical slate hanging to their cheeks. Re-modelled in 1952 by architect Geoffrey Drewitt Alterations included the full-length bay window and doorway to the front elevation and revised layout of the interior at ground floor level.

42 **FORMER WESLYAN METHODIST CHAPEL, GARRISON LANE**

[SV 902106]

1825. (Opened in 1828). Two-storey building which was renovated in 1883-84. Walls are constructed with coursed granite rubble and ashlar to two facades. The slate hipped roof covering has been replaced with asbestos sheeting but the original substantial roof timbers survive above a suspended ceiling at first floor level. Internally. angled staircases lead up to U-plan panel-fronted galleries on the first floor which are supported on cast-iron Tuscan columns. The forecourt walls and railings were added in 1926. The building was superseded in 1899 and is now disused. In about 1790, it replaced the original Wesleyan Chapel which was built on the same site.

43 EIGHT TERRACE HOUSES & SHOP, SOUTH SIDE, HUGH STREET

[SV 902106]

c.1926. Designed by architects Richardson and Gill for the Duchy of Cornwall, replacing an earlier informal row of houses and cottages. Two storeys built with coursed and dressed granite and flat concrete roofs. Relieved by careful proportions and subtle detailing to plinths, pilasters, parapets and recessed chimney stacks. The corner entrance to the shop is emphasised by its special treatment.

44 POST OFFICE, HUGH STREET

[SV 902106]

1897. Probably designed by Thomas Algernon Dorrien-Smith, 'Lord Proprietor' and amateur architect. Unusual style, almost Alpine. Innovative use of materials as seen in other examples of Dorrien-Smith's estate architecture. Snecked rock-faced granite with shaped boulder-faced granite surrounds and dressings used to the front elevation. Massive hewn boulders specified for cills, quoins and lintels around openings and rough granite used for window mullions. Slate covered roofs have two projecting gables of different sizes, with cantilevered granite brackets and scissor trusses. A segmental arch spans the carriageway leading to Well Lane.

45 KAVORNA BAKERY & SHOP, HUGH STREET, SOUTH SIDE

[SV 902106]

18th-19th century with 20th century alterations. Possibly two dwellings originally. The two-storey building now used as a shop and a flat. Coursed granite rubble with painted render to front facade and slate roof. L-plan with 18th century rear wing to one side. 20th century shop windows have been inserted to the front of the ground floor.

46 LLOYDS BANK, HUGH STREET

[SV 901106]

Mid-19th century. Formerly a house. Built in granite rubble with painted render. Classical order used for front porch with its two Roman Doric columns, Doric antae, entablature and cornice. An important element in the townscape which encloses the space to its forecourt and the adjacent buildings whilst providing a useful interruption to the vista down Hugh Street from Silver Street.

47 COTTAGES, SOUTH WEST SIDE, THE BANK

[SV 901106]

c.18th and 19th centuries. A footpath leading down from Jerusalem Terrace to Hugh Street separates a row of three 18th century cottages from a further 18th and 19th century cottage and adjoining house built on the southern corner of the Bank. Materials used for these two-storey buildings include granite rubble walls painted white, rendered granite chimney stacks and various types of slate roofs.

48 HOUSES AND SHOPS, NORTH WEST SIDE, THE BANK

[SV 901107]

Late 18th-early 19th century. Two-storey shops and houses built in coursed granite with slate roofs. Details include bay windows, brick chimney stacks and a dormer window with a curved sash window.

49 TWO HOUSES, WEST SIDE, THE BANK

[SV 901107]

c.18th century. Two dwellings overlooking the Bank which were restored and altered in the early 20th century. Built with granite rubble with painted finish to both fairfaced and rendered granite walls. A number of interesting features include double height bay windows and bow windows.

50 TWO HOUSES, SOUTH SIDE, GARRISON HILL

[SV 901107]

c.17th-19th century. Stepping up the steep hill these two dwellings are illustrated by Richardson and Gill in *Regional Architecture of the West of England*. The higher building is believed to date from much earlier, (possibly Tudor), than the lower one. Built in granite with slate roofs they mark the approach to Garrison Gate and its important fortifications.

51 THE GUARDHOUSE, GARRISON GATE

[SV 901107]

Early 17th century. Formerly a guard room but now used as a house it was heightened to two storeys, probably during the 18th century. Built with roughly coursed granite rubble walls and gabled slate roof. The door and windows have replaced earlier joinery. The imposing Garrison Gate adjacent to the Guardhouse was built in the late 16th-early 17th century. It was rebuilt in 1742 by Abraham Tovey when the bellcote was added. A plaque depicts Tovey's initials and the date of the reconstruction.

52 **GATEHOUSE COTTAGE**

[SV 901107]

Late 16th-early 17th century with a later 17th century extension to the right hand side and a 20th century extension for the rear outshut. A single-¿storey building with hipped dormers serving the attic Formerly it was used as a store for the barracks but now adapted to form a dwelling. Walls are built in roughly coursed granite with dressed granite blocks to the right hand extension. The gabled slate roof has carved finials to the stone copings. Door and window joinery is 19th century.

53 **ROCKET HOUSE**

[SV 900107]

Early 17th century. Re-modelled powder magazine and blast walls with adjoining prison hole which now houses an English Heritage display on the history of Scilly's fortifications. Coursed granite blocks are used for the walls in conjunction with a steeply pitched slate roof and a stone ridge. Segmental-arched entry to magazine and blast walls. Ventilation ports are formed in the walls to the magazine and there is an internal vaulted stone roof.

54 **GARRISON HOUSE**

[SV 900107]

18th century. Two-storey dwelling built with squared and coursed granite blocks and slate

roofs which are half-hipped on one side and hipped over outshut to the other side. 20th century alterations include doors and windows and large dormer window to the outshut.

55 **VERONICA LODGE, THE GARRISON**

[SV 906101]

c.1790. Two-storey house built for the Commanding Officer of the Garrison. Painted render finish to granite rubble walls and a hipped slate roof. Porch to the semi-circular arched doorway dates from the mid 20th century.

56 **HUGH HOUSE, THE GARRISON**

[SV 905101]

1792. Originally used as an Officer's Mess for the Garrison and later, in 1835, as Augustus Smith's first residence.Subsequently it was converted into a hotel and today it provides offices for the Duchy of Cornwall. Three-storey with imposing symmetrical front elevation in granite ashlar. Central hall and staircase. Coursed granite rubble used elsewhere with slate hung side walls, gabled slate roof and granite chimney stacks. Interior remodelled in 20th century although 19th

century panelled doors have been retained. Pedimented front doorway is also a 20th century addition.

57 **TRINITY COTTAGES, THE GARRISON**

[SV 901103]

1858. Two pairs of two-storey houses built by Trinity House for lighthouse keepers on the Garrison Walk overlooking Porthcressa. Design typical to similar buildings found on the mainland with white painted render to granite walls Distinguished by symmetrical openings, stone copings to gables, slate covered roofs and porches.

58 **SIGNAL GUN TOWER, THE GARRISON**

[SV 898103]

Late 16th- early 17th century. One of a pair, this surviving building was originally a Windmill Tower which was converted into a gun tower in 1803 to the design of Major Daniel Lyman. After further alterations and conversion it is now used as a single residence. Circular on plan, the tower is built with roughly coursed granite rubble walls

and granite lintels over wall openings and a parapet wall at roof level.

59 **STAR CASTLE, THE GARRISON**

[SV 899107]

1593 with late 17th century alterations. Designed by architect-engineer Robert Adams. Star Castle has served as a fort, governor's residence and a prison but it has been used as a hotel since 1933. The star-shaped eight-sided plan contains a two-storey dwelling and defines its central keep, curtain wall and dry moat. Built in rendered granite rubble with granite and brick dressings and an M-shaped hipped roof of slurried slate. Flat roofed dormers serve the attic spaces. This is the main fort in a defensive system built under Francis Godolphin to counter the threat posed by the Spanish after the Armada in 1588. Star Castle is an important and complete example of an Elisabethan fort built to a common Renaissance plan. The present building has retained many of its original features.

60 NEWMAN HOUSE, THE GARRISON

[SV 899108]

1716-1718. Originally known as Store House Battery and named after the Garrison store and the workshops behind it. The addition of the porch and internal alterations in 1927 are by architects Richardson and Gill. This impressive and important two-storey building with attics, now a private house, was restored in 1971. Materials include coursed granite rubble, dressed granite, slates to roofs and dormer cheeks and stone copings. A variety of interesting details include segmental arches with dressed voussoirs and keystones to openings, coved cornices, hipped dormers and sash windows with curved heads.

61 THE WHITE HOUSE, THE GARRISON

[SV 900107]

Mid 18th century. Built for Master Gunner Abraham Tovey, this two-storey house has been subject to extensive alterations and re-modelling. Walls are built in rendered granite painted white whilst the roof covering is now cement slates.

62 PIER HOUSE, WEST SIDE, HUGH STREET

[SV 901107]

c.17th century. Opposite to the Mermaid public house. Two-storey house with attics remodelled in the early 19th century. The earlier house was single-storey, evidence of its steeply pitched roof being apparent from the wall to the gable end. Random coursed granite walls, lintels and chimney stacks with slate roofs.

63 TERRACE HOUSES, NORTH SIDE, HUGH STREET

[SV 902107]

Late 18th century. Formerly terrace of four houses now used as flats, houses and shops. Materials include coursed and squared granite, painted render, flat roofs behind granite parapets and granite chimney stacks. Features include late 19th century shopfront with colonettes and arched spandrels.

64 HOUSE, NORTH SIDE, HUGH STREET

[SV 907102]

c.18th century. Two-storey end house with attic built adjacent to the slipway. Coursed and squared granite walls with a gabled slate roof. A 20th century extension with a flat roof has been added to the rear.

65 ATLANTIC HOTEL, NORTH SIDE, HUGH STREET

[SV 902106]

Late 18th and 19th century. Remodelled in 1927 by architects Richardson and Gill for the Duchy of Cornwall. Coursed and squared granite walls. Natural and artificial slate roofs. Gables to rear wings and half-hipped roof to corner of front elevation. Vertical slate hanging to dormer cheeks. Central doorway with Greek revival pilasters. Interior re-designed but retains open fireplaces with granite lintels. The building embraces the former custom house of 1840.

66 **BARCLAYS BANK, NORTH SIDE, HUGH STREET**

[SV 902106]

1935. Designed by architect Frederick Drewitt, the walls and pilasters are rendered and painted white with granite plinths and quoins. The entrance is carefully detailed; the door being placed in a wider recess with fluted columns. The windows are symmetrically placed either side of the entrance in semi-circular headed recesses with half-dormer windows above and a pitched artificial slate roof. The bank adjoins an undistinguished shop on one side.

67 **SCILLONIAN STEAMSHIP OFFICES, NORTH SIDE, HUGH STREET**

[SV 902106]

1939. Two-storey office building designed by Martin, architect for the Duchy of Cornwall. Fairfaced granite ashlar walls used to the front elevation of the ground floor and natural rendered granite walls to floor above. An unusual detail is the use of circular granite columns at street level.

68 **SHOP, NORTH SIDE, THE PARADE**

[SV 903106]

Early - mid 19th century. Two-storey building with coursed granite rubble walls, granite lintels and half-hipped slate roof. The building, together with the adjacent restaurant at right angles to it and the Bishop and Wolf public house opposite, form an important part of the townscape enclosing a small square at the junction of four narrow streets.

69 **HOUSE, NORTH SIDE, THE PARADE**

[SV 903106]

Late 18th-early 19th century. Three-storey with cellar below. Walls built in coursed granite rubble, with fairfaced stucco to the front elevation. Interlocking concrete tiles to main half-hipped roof and slates to roof of rear wing.

70 BORDEAUX SHOP, NORTH SIDE, THE PARADE

[SV 903106]

Early 19th century. with later alterations. Two-storey house and shop built in roughly coursed granite with painted render to front elevation and gabled slate roof Early 19th century shop front with reeded pilasters, and frieze with cornice framing.

71 STANMORE HOUSE, N. SIDE THE PARADE

[SV 903106]

Early 19th century. Two-storey building with coursed granite walls and late 20th century interlocking concrete tiles to half-hipped roof. Granite lintels above sash windows and semi-circular arch with granite voussoirs above door opening.

72 THE GALLEY AND GALLEY RESTAURANT, NORTH SIDE, THE PARADE

[SV 903105]

Early 19th century. Two-storey house with shop attached. Painted render to roughly coursed granite rubble walls Gabled slate roof

and rendered chimney stacks. Late 19th century shop window with pilaster strips and frieze with cornice.

73 COTTAGES, NORTH SIDE, THE PARADE

[SV 903106]

c. 18th -19th century. Picturesque row of two-storey cottages overlooking the Park in the centre of Hugh Town. 19th century outshuts and mid-20th century extensions to the rear. Granite rubble walls with painted render to frontages. Gabled slate roofs and mid-20th century doors and windows.

74 PAIR OF HOUSES, NORTH SIDE, THE PARADE

[SV 904106]

Early 19th century. with earlier origins. Two-storey with walls constructed in coursed and roughly dressed granite, one house being finished with painted render. Half-hipped slate roof with rendered ridge and rear chimney stacks. Late 19th century sash windows and doorways with half columns. Left return wall of one house has quoins to centre indicating the rear wall of an earlier house which was increased in depth and heightened.

75 HOUSES AND SHOP, EAST SIDE, THE PARADE

[SV 904105]

Early 18th and early 19th century. Two-storey houses with shop which have been subject to later 19th alterations. Coursed granite rubble walls and gabled slate roofs, part slurried. Hipped dormer windows serve attic spaces to one house.

76 STRAND HOUSE AND CUSTOM HOUSE, NORTH SIDE, LOWER STRAND

[SV 904106]

Early 19th century. Partially remodelled in 1927 by architects Richardson and Gill for the Duchy of Cornwall when the custom house was moved from the rear of the Atlantic Hotel. Originally two houses, now used as a guest house, custom house and club. Materials used include coursed granite rubble walls with painted render finish, rusticated quoins and slates for the roofs. Granite steps and decorative iron railings, dating from 1810, have been retained.

77 ROMAN CATHOLIC CHURCH, LOWER STRAND

[SV 904106]

1860. Originally St Mary's Girls School and established as part of Augustus Smith's commitment to the cause of education on all of the Islands. The AS monogram and date is indicated on the front facade. The first floor of the two-storey building, which was originally a classroom, now serves as the Roman Catholic chapel of Our Lady - Stella Maris. 'Star of the Sea'. The church also provides accommodation for the priest. Pleasant rear courtyard.

78 LYONESSE HOUSE, SOUTH SIDE, LOWER STRAND

[SV 904106]

1830 Regency style facade with earlier house behind. Three-storey house built in coursed random rubble with a painted render finish. Parapet conceals slate roof and rendered chimney stacks. Details include sash windows, plain Doric pilasters and entablature to front doorway, half-glazed inner porch door and stick-baluster staircase.

79 TEN TERRACE COTTAGES, HIGHER STRAND

[SV 905106]

Early-mid 19th century. Two-storey but with three end cottages being taller and built at a later date. Coursed granite rubble walls with granite lintels over door and window openings. Slate roofs with rendered granite ridges and chimney stacks. Generally late 19th or 20th century replacement windows and doors.

80 LIFEBOAT HOUSE, CARN THOMAS

[SV 906108]

1900. Built with a deep-water slipway to house a new lifeboat. Constructed with coursed granite walls and natural slate roof, the building projects out of the rocky promontory at Carn Thomas. Another replacement lifeboat in 1980 was unsuitable for launching down the slipway and had to be kept afloat at permanent moorings but the lifeboat house is still used to accommodate the lifeboat tender and exhibits.

81 SCHOOL, CARN THOMAS

[SV 907107]

1854. Boys' Primary School designed by Augustus Smith. Materials used include coursed rubble granite walls and concrete tiled roofs with rendered block walls and artificial roof slates to the large 20th century extension. Details include AS monogram, and bell housing.

82 **SECONDARY SCHOOL, CARN THOMAS**

[SV 907106]

1966. Built in two phases. Initial phase by architect Geoffrey Bazeley and the second phase by project architect John Massey for Cornwall's County Architect. Two-storey building with first floor cantilevered over footpath. Design is typical of schools built on the mainland at that time based on the ideas of the 20th century modern movement and the new approach to secondary education.

83 **COTTAGES, TELEGRAPH ROAD, PORTH MELLON**

[SV 908107]

Late 19th-early 20th century. Several two-storey cottages built in this area of St Mary's using local granite for their walls and imported slates, either natural or artificial for their roofs.

84 **COTTAGE OFF TELEGRAPH ROAD**

[SV 911108]

19th century. Picturesque two-storey cottage which uses traditional materials including granite and slates. Attractive landscaping appropriate for its setting.

85 **TERRACE HOUSES, PORTHLOO**

[SV 909113]

1925-30. Two-storey houses which were designed for the Duchy of Cornwall. The use of granite for the walls, sash windows and flat roofs is similar to specification for contemporary terraced houses built on behalf of the Duchy at Longstone on St Mary's and in Hugh Street.

86 **RESTAURANT, PORTHLOO**

[SV 908116]

c. 18th - early 19th century. Architects Poynton Bradbury and Winter. Part of a vernacular farm complex, namely Seaways Flower Farm. Formerly an agricultural barn used for bulb packing and storage, the ground floor is still being used for this purpose. Conversion and extension in traditional style with timber framing and cladding to a kitchen extension. Exposed timber roof trusses to new restaurant and red clay roof pantiles. Superb views from the terrace and restaurant overlooking the Pool at Hugh Town and the Off-Islands.

87 TELEGRAPH TOWER

[SV 912121]

1803. One of three gun towers proposed and built on St Mary's by Major Daniel Lyman. Situated on the highest point of the islands, 165 feet above sea level, the building is now used as a coastguard's Look-out Tower. Circular on plan and four storeys high it is constructed with coursed shaped granite blocks. Upper floors are slightly set back from the projecting ground floor and the flat roof is surrounded by a parapet with string courses below. In 1898 Guglielmo Marconi is reported to have heard wireless signals at this tower from about thirty miles away at Porthcurno in Cornwall.

88 COTTAGE, WATERMILL LANE

[SV 919120]

c.18th century. Extended in 1832 and again in the late 18th-early 19th century. Two storeys. Roughly coursed granite used for the older section of the building with coursed roughly dressed granite to the 1832 extension. Roofs covered with artificial slates. Windows dating from 18th, 19th and 20th centuries. Noted as a good example of a multi-period Scillonian house.

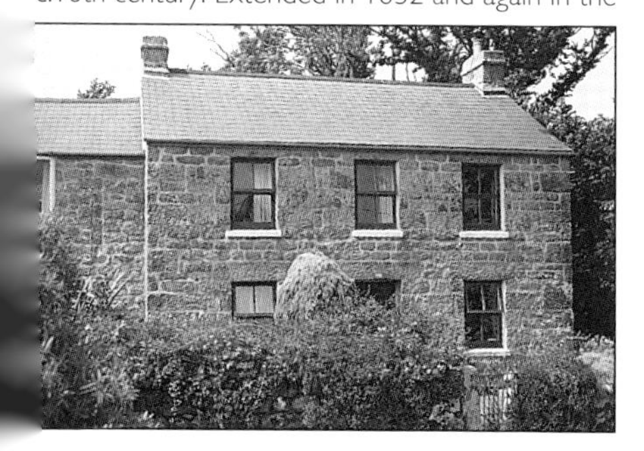

89 BOROUGH FARM

[SV 920119]

Late 18th - early 19th century. Two-storey farmhouse with various outbuildings. Walls built with squared random course granite and slurried slate roof. Central granite gabled porch and stone chimney stacks. Roof to left hand 19th century wing of the house is covered with red pantiles.

90 COTTAGE AT PELISTRY FARM

[SV 924118]

18th-19th century. Two-storey cottage with outshut which has recently been carefully restored. Constructed with painted random rubble and artificial slate roof. 20th century timber replacement sash windows.

91 **COTTAGES AT HOLY VALE**

[SV 920115]
c.18th-early 19th century with 20th century alterations including inappropriate timber replacement windows. Attractive and historic location.

92 **TERRACE HOUSES, TELEGRAPH ROAD, LONGSTONE**

[SV 917112]
1925-30. Two-storey terrace houses with flat roofs built for the Duchy of Cornwall. Description similar to terrace houses at Porthloo.

93 **AIRPORT TERMINAL BUILDING**

[SV 918104]
1975. Opened by the late Sir Harold Wilson and extended 1988-89. A further extension in 1994 was opened by H.R.H Duchess of Kent. The original building was designed by architect R. E. Nugent for British European Airways. Built with fairfaced concrete block walls and exposed timber beams and rafters supporting concrete tiled roofs. An honest response to the brief for a 20th century building type which accepted the challenge of providing an important landmark on a prominent site overlooking Old Town.

94 **LAUNCESTON CLOSE, OLD TOWN**

[SV 914102]
1966. Designed by Louis De Soissons' architectural practice, well-known for their innovative approach to housing at Welwyn Garden City in Hertfordshire. This two-storey housing scheme for the Duchy of Cornwall follows the general principles of the practice's earlier housing schemes in respect of layout, vehicular access and attention to materials and detailing but the scheme lacks the potential offered by its location and context.

95 **RESTAURANT AND BAR, OLD TOWN**

[SV 914104]
c. 18th - 19th century. Single -storey barns sympathetically converted into a bar, skittle alley and restaurant in 1995.

96 **COTTAGES, OLD TOWN**

[SV 914104]
c. 18th-early 19th century. A pleasing group of two-storey terraced cottages and detached two-storey cottages built in granite with artificial slate roofs which have been subject to improvements but retained many of their original features.

97 **PRIMARY SCHOOL, OLD TOWN**

[SV 911103]
1977. Opened by H.R.H. Prince Charles, Duke of Cornwall. Designed by the Cornwall County Architect's Department (project architect John Matthews). A interesting series of pavilions with mono-pitched roofs grouped around open courts and playground areas. The School successfully harmonises with its setting without resorting to mimicking the form and materials of

the traditional buildings on Scilly. Blockwork walls are rendered and painted whilst the roofs are covered with interlocking concrete tiles. The hard and soft landscaping has been carefully considered.

98 OLD CHURCH OF ST MARY, OLD TOWN

[SV 911100]

1662, rebuilt c.1830 and restored 1890. Single cell plan with north porch. Built with roughly coursed rubble granite with ashlar dressings, slate covered roofs with stone copings. The setting of this church overlooking the cove is of outstanding beauty. Augustus Smith landscaped the churchyard; obelisks provide memorials to him and Louise Holzmaister, one of the passengers lost from the shipwrecked S.S. Schiller. Victims of the Schiller and the Association are buried in this peaceful haven. Lord Wilson, the former Prime Minister is also buried here.

99 PENINNIS LIGHTHOUSE

[SV 911094]

1911. Situated on Peninnis Headland which is about 110 feet above sea level. The structure is a steel trestle tower with the upper part plated to form a service room below the lantern. The steel gallery below the lantern is 30 feet above ground level. It was originally lit by oil gas and subsequently converted to operate on compressed acetylene gas in 1920. Evidence of the concrete supports which used to support the old oil gas tanks can still be seen in the station's compound.

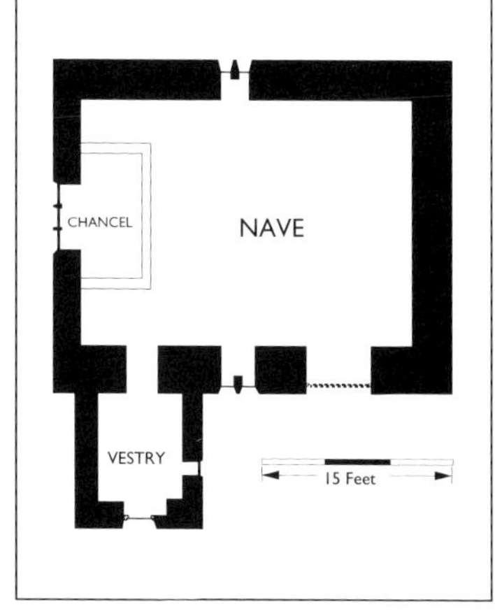

100 **HOSPITAL**

[SV 907104]

1939. A plain functional building with rendered walls painted white and pitched roofs. Designed by Guy Aldis of Geoffrey Bazeley, architects.

101 **BUZZA TOWER, BUZZA HILL, HUGH TOWN**

[SV 906104]

1821. Disused windmill used for grinding corn built on the site of a cairn excavated by Borlase. Restored 1911 in commemoration of visit of Edward VII. Circular plan on three storeys with ground floor veranda and slate roof supported on iron posts and granite pillars. Built in squared and coursed granite with parapet wall to slate roof.

ST AGNES

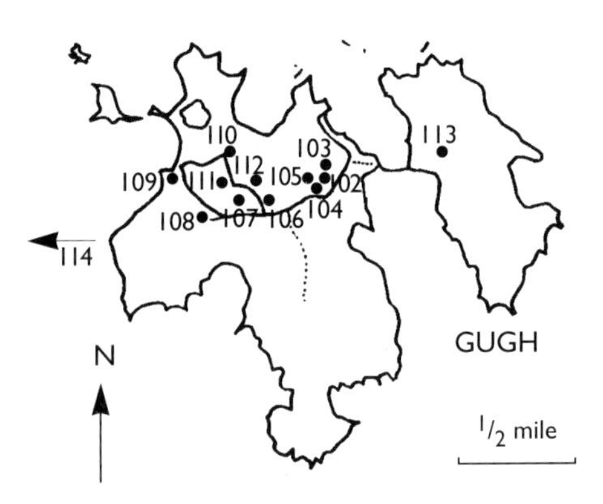

102 **ROSE COTTAGE & TEA GARDEN, HIGHER TOWN**

[SV 884083]

18th century (rear wing) with 19th century extension and 20th century flat-roofed extension. 'L' plan to two-storey section and single -storey rear wing with hipped roof. Built in roughly coursed granite, slurried slate roof and brick chimneys. There are fine views to the south from the sheltered garden.

103 **HOUSE AT HIGHER TOWN**

[SV 884083]

Early 19th century. Two storeys constructed in roughly coursed granite with artificial slate roof and granite chimney stacks. Central lean-to glazed entrance porch and timber sash windows.

104 COTTAGE, HIGHER TOWN

[SV 883082]

Late 18th - early 19th century. Two-storey building which was originally a farmhouse. Built in roughly coursed granite rubble colourwashed white, with outshuts to both the side and rear. Cement slate roofs and rendered granite chimney stacks.

105 COTTAGE, HIGHER TOWN

[SV 883083]

18th century. Two-storey building formerly a farmhouse. Late 19th century alterations included raising the eaves to increase the height. Walls built with roughly coursed granite rubble. Slurried Delabole slate roof and granite chimney stacks. Late 19th century glazed shed built for the flower industry. Complete Scillonian interior includes beaded plank partitions, mid-19th century fireplace and additional kitchen fireplace.

106 ANNET FARMBUILDING, MIDDLETOWN

[SV 881082]

Early 19th century. Formerly used as a threshing barn, cowhouse and stables. Two storeys with shutters to first floor loft doors above granite lintels over outer doorways. Originally housed threshing machine. Building materials include

roughly coursed granite rubble walls and corrugated asbestos roof. A good example of an advanced type of farmbuilding which was built when St Agnes was noted for its fertile corn-bearing soil.

107 ST AGNES LIGHTHOUSE, HOUSE AND ANCILLARY BUILDING

[SV 880082]

1680. Three -storey lighthouse plus a fourth -storey cupola and ancillary building (c.1840) erected for Trinity House. The lighthouse is about 60 feet tall and built at a height of 200 feet above high-water mark. Circular on plan and constructed with white colourwashed render on granite rubble walls surmounted by a cast iron and glass cupola dated 1806. Single-storey lean-to porch and corridor attached to a passagelinked to the adjacent house built in 1840. A stone mural stair provides access to the first floor which has four gun ports. A wooden newel stair from the shallow stone vaulted first floor leads up to the lantern. A plaque inside the building records that it was built by Captain Hugh Till and Captain Simon Bayly. The light was originally supplied by a coal fire and later by an oil lamp. The original iron cresset is now in Tresco gardens. Picturesque 'H' plan Tudor style house. Built in colourwashed render on granite rubble walls with slate roofs and octagonal flues to chimney stacks. Hipped slate roof to ancillary building.

108
COASTGUARD HOUSES
[SV 879081]
c.1929. Built incorrectly with the watchtower facing inland instead of over the Western Rocks. White painted rendered granite walls. Distinguished by symmetrical window openings, stone copings to gables, steep pitched roofs and porches covered with artificial slates.

109 ST AGNES CHURCH
[SV 878083]
1821. Preceded by two earlier churches. before the end of the 18th. century. Comprises a lean-to porch on the south side, panelled internal gallery and a small low tower to the west end. Semi-circular arched east window and square-headed 20th century windows to the side walls.

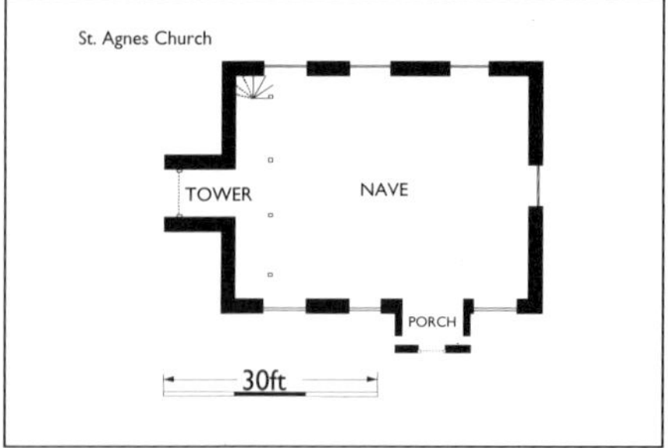

110 LOWER TOWN FARM
[SV 879084]
18th-early 19th century. Two storey farmhouse built in roughly coursed granite. 20th century extension painted white with artificial and natural slates to 'M' shaped roof.

111 COTTAGES, MIDDLE TOWN
[SV 870083]
Late 18th-early 19th century. Two detached two-storey cottages built in roughly coursed granite, one fairface and one painted white. Artificial slate roofs and rendered granite chimneys.

112 THE PARSONAGE
[SV 881082]
Early 19th century. Two-torey building, formerly a parsonage and now used as a house. Colourwashed render on granite rubble with slate roofs and rendered brick chimney stacks Attractive landscaped setting.

113 TWO HOUSES ON GUGH
[SV 889084]
c.1920 with later additions. Built by Cooper, a retired London Borough Surveyor, they are

distinguished by their unconventional sweeping concrete roofs which were designed to resist damage due to lifting in severe gales. The walls of both houses are built with granite,one house being rendered and painted white.

114 BISHOP ROCK LIGHTHOUSE

[SV 807065]

c. 1852 - 1858 The tallest and best-known lighthouse in the British Isles. Designed by James Walker together with the earlier ill-fated iron tower which was swept away in a storm. Sir James Nicholas Tregarthen accompanied his father Nicholas Douglass in building the lighthouse who designed the later reconstruction and strengthening of Bishop Rock in 1882 when William Tregarthen Douglass acted as resident engineer.

BRYHER

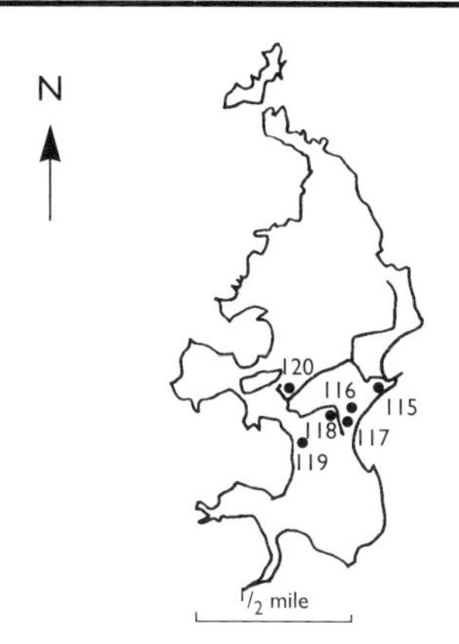

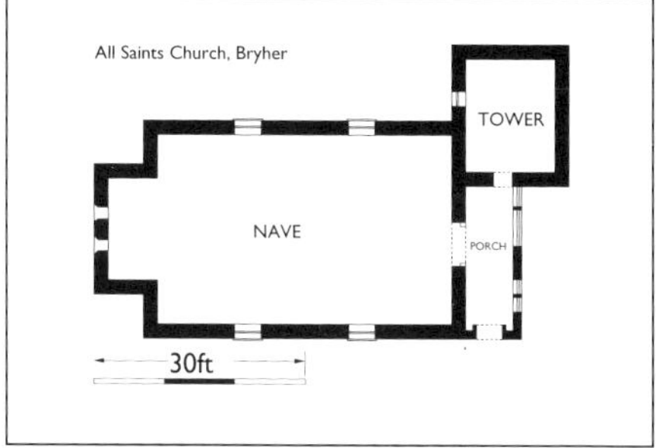

115 CHURCH OF ALL SAINTS

[SV 880149]

1742. Dedicated to 'God and All Saints' by the Reverend P. Hathaway on 21 November 1740. The church also served the community on the nearby island of Samson when it was inhabited. Originally it only measured 13 feet by 24 feet. Additions and alterations were carried out in 1882 and 1897. Now comprises of nave, narrowed sanctuary, porch and a south-west tower with a pyramidal roof. The line of an earlier roof pitch can be seen on the west gable end. The stained glass windows are late 19th century. The plain granite font is dated 1861. A plaque inside from the Society for the Protection of Churches, states that the building had been rebuilt and enlarged in 1882 to provide 94 seats in lieu of the former 60.

116 VERONICA FARMHOUSE
[SV 878147]
Early 19th century with later 19th century extension. Formerly a farmhouse but now used as a house. Two storeys built with roughly coursed granite rubble with larger blocks of granite to the later extension. Slate roofs to both main range and extension. Rendered chimney stacks. Interior re-modelled in 20th century. Associated with the brewhouse below.

117 BREWHOUSE
[SV 87147]
19th century. Dr Borlase noted in the 18th century that almost every house on the islands was undertaking milling corn by hand and brewing. Single-storey building with loft. Materials used include roughly coursed granite for the walls and pantiles for the roof. Granite lintel used over wall openings and fireplace. Four nailed A-frame roof trusses.

118 THE FORGE
[SV 878148]
18th century. Single storey outbuilding, formerly a house. Built with roughly coursed granite walls pantile roof. Granite lintels over door and window openings and granite chimney stacks. A rare surviving example of a single-storey dwelling, a type once prevalent on the islands before the 19th century brought higher standards of living.

119 ARTIST'S STUDIO
[SV 876147]
c. 1870. Gig shed for the Golden Eagle. Converted into artist's studio in 1994 using driftwood for floors, roof members and fittings.

120 COTTAGE, GREAT PORTH
[SV 876148]
Late 18th-early 19th century. Picturesque cottage illustrated in a painting by local artist John Hamilton. Granite walls to main building and porch. 20th century slate roofs with rendered granite chimney stacks.

FURTHER READING

Borlase, W. ***Observations on the Ancient and Present State of the Islands of Scilly*** (1756)
Bowley, R.L. ***The Fortunate Islands*** (1980)
Brunskill, ***Vernacular Architecture*** (1971)
Cornwall Archaeological Unit. ***Scilly's Archaeological Heritage*** (1992)
Cornwall Archaeological Unit. Berry, E. & Ratcliffe, J. ***The Samsom Buildings*** (1994)
Cornwall County Council. ***The Garrison. A Walk around the Walls.***
Department of the Environment. ***Ancient Monuments of the Isles of Scilly*** (1949)
Dorrien Smith, C. ***Tresco Abbey***
Forrester Matthews, G. ***The Isles of Scilly*** (1960)
Hague, D.B. & Christie, R. ***Lighthouses, Their Architecture, History and Archaeology*** (1975)
Inglis-Jones, E. ***Augustus Smith of Scilly*** (1969)
Laws, P. ***The Buildings of Scilly*** (1980)
Mothershole, J. ***The Isles of Scilly. Their Story, their Folk, their Flowers*** (1910)
Over. L. ***The Isles of Scilly*** (1993)
Pevsner N. & Radcliffe E. ***Cornwall*** (1951)
Richardson, & Gill, ***The Regional Architecture of the West of England*** (1924)
Tarrant, M. ***Cornwall's Lighthouse Heritage*** (1990)

ISBN 0906294 36 3

First published 1996 by Twelveheads Press, Chy Mengleth, Twelveheads, Truro, Cornwall TR4 8SN.